JUNK FOOD FOR THOUGHT

SWEET STORIES ABOUT CANDY

KENNY ABDO

Fly!
An Imprint of Abdo Zoom
abdobooks.com

abdobooks.com

Published by Abdo Zoom, a division of ABDO, P.O. Box 398166, Minneapolis, Minnesota 55439.

Printed in the United States of America, North Mankato, Minnesota.
052025
092025

Photo Credits: AdobeStock, Alamy, Getty Images, Shutterstock
Production Contributors: Kenny Abdo, Jennie Forsberg, Grace Hansen
Design Contributors: Candice Keimig, Neil Klinepier, Laura Graphenteen

Library of Congress Control Number: 2024947740

Publisher's Cataloging-in-Publication Data

Names: Abdo, Kenny, author.
Title: Sweet stories about candy / by Kenny Abdo
Description: Minneapolis, Minnesota : Abdo Zoom, 2026 | Series: Junk food for thought | Includes online resources and index.
Identifiers: ISBN 9781098288815 (lib. bdg.) | ISBN 9781098289515 (ebook) | ISBN 9781098289867 (Read-to-me ebook)
Subjects: LCSH: Junk food--Juvenile literature. | Food technology--Juvenile literature. | Food additives--Juvenile literature. | Candies--Juvenile literature. | Processed foods--Juvenile literature.
Classification: DDC 641.853--dc23

TABLE OF CONTENTS

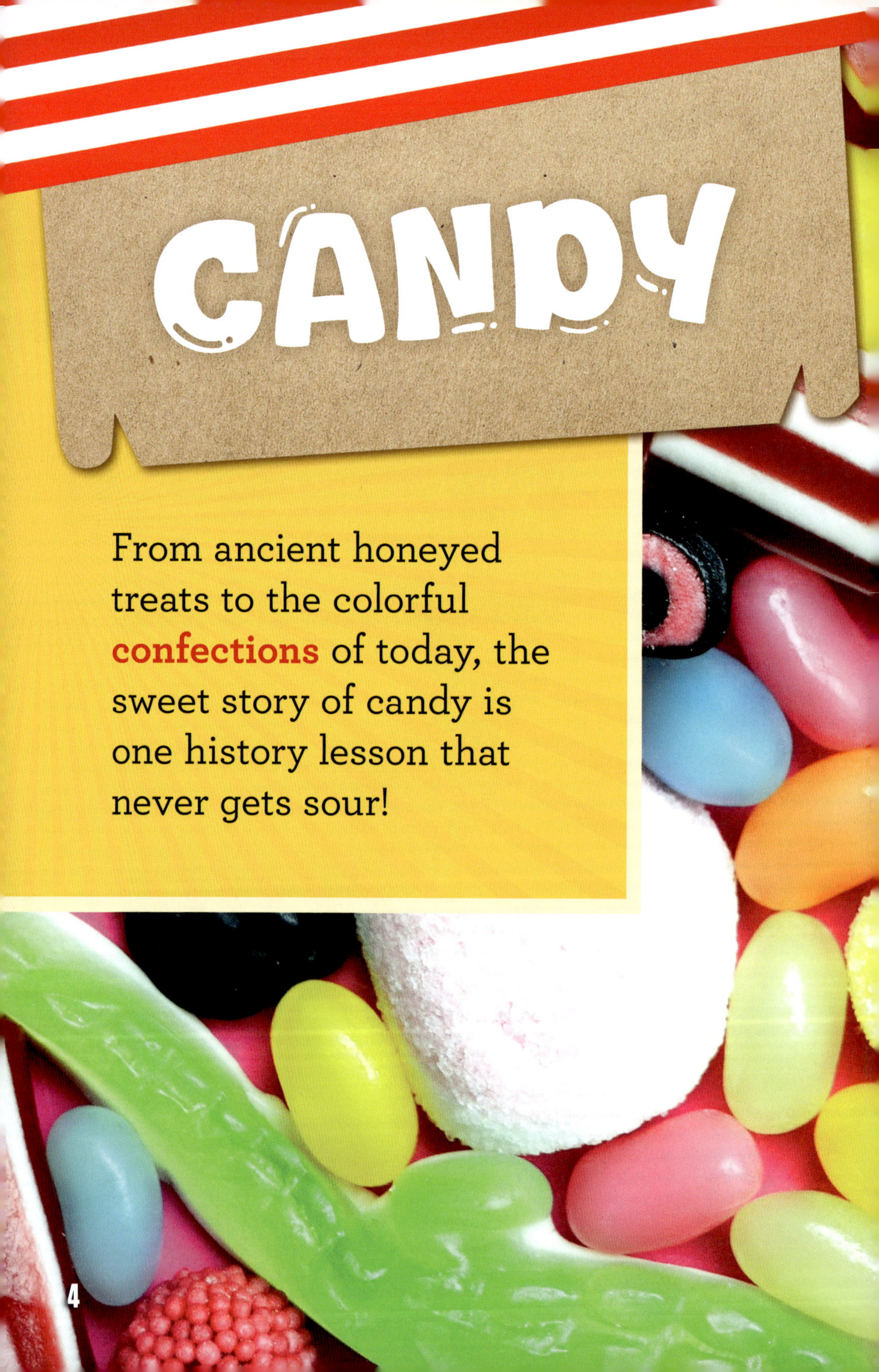

CANDY

From ancient honeyed treats to the colorful **confections** of today, the sweet story of candy is one history lesson that never gets sour!

THE EARLY JUNK

The folks in ancient Egypt made candy with honey, nuts, and fruits. They even used candy in religious **rituals** because they thought it was special. Honey made the candy sweet and helped keep it fresh.

In the mid-1600s, King Christian V of Denmark was sick with throat pains. He did not like the medicine the doctor gave him. The doctor blended it with sugar and a small amount of beetroot juice. It hardened and the King loved it. Hard candy was born! With new flavors like peppermint, candy canes **debuted** in 1847.

THE FOOD PROCESS JUNK

In 1907, the Hershey Company introduced Hershey's Kisses. The small, foil-wrapped chocolates quickly became candy lovers' one and only. Hershey's named them Kisses because of the sound they made during production. Just a year later, George Smith slapped a piece of hard candy on a stick. He named his creation after a local racehorse, Lolly Pop.

In 1922, German **confectioner** Hans Riegel was inspired while attending a festival where he watched trained dancing bears. The sight led him to his next hit candy. Riegel quickly introduced the first gummy bears. His candy company, Haribo, continues to sell the gummies today!

During **World War II**, soldiers appreciated Tootsie Rolls because they were easy to carry and would not melt. After the war, their popularity continued as people appreciated them, too. In 1950, PEZ dispensers **debuted**. They held mint candies and were geared toward adults. But kids loved the fun designs. They even became a collector's item.

PEZ
LEMON
PEZ
GRAPE
RASPBERRY
PEZ
NATURALLY FLAVORED
PEZ
ORANGE

Fruits

In the 1960s, Starburst came to the US from the UK. Initially called Opal Fruits, the chewy candy came in flavors like lemon, lime, strawberry, and orange. SweeTarts also became popular around this time. People loved their sweet and sour taste.

People's taste for candy continued to sour into the 1970s, but in a good way! Candy maker Frank Galatolie first created small sour candies called Mars Men. However, when Cabbage Patch Kids became a worldwide sensation, the Mars Men left space to become Sour Patch Kids. And, the rest is bittersweet history!

The 1980s were a sweet time for candy. In 1981, Haribo introduced sour gummy worms, giving gummy candy a tangy twist. In 1982, Reese's Pieces became famous after being featured in the movie *E.T. the Extra-Terrestrial*. Both candies are still going strong today.

In the 1990s, candy started to get extreme. Pop Rocks made your mouth fizz, Skittles allowed people to "taste the rainbow," and Gushers, which had gooey centers, came out in 1991. Then, in 1993, Warheads took over with their super sour flavors. These candies became classic '90s treats.

Fruits
Skittles
Fruits
Skittles

In the 2000s, candy makers got really creative. They made chocolate-covered potato chips. This sweet and salty treat sparked more candy experiments, creating new flavors and combinations.

THE TUMMY ACHE

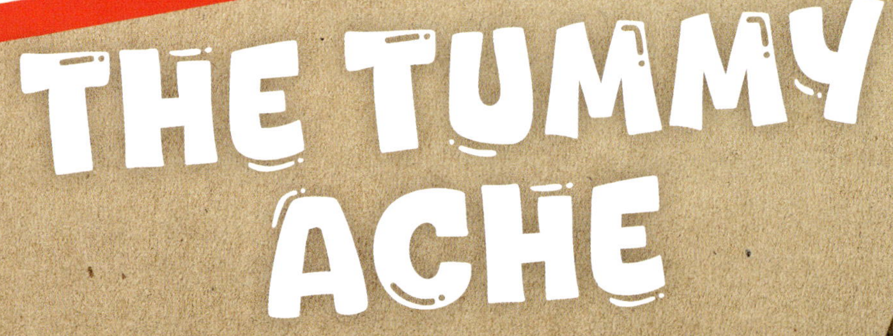

By the 2010s, companies such as Alter Eco and Endangered Species Chocolate started making candy with **organic** ingredients and **eco-friendly** packaging, aiming to make candy that's not just tasty but **sustainable** for the planet, as well.

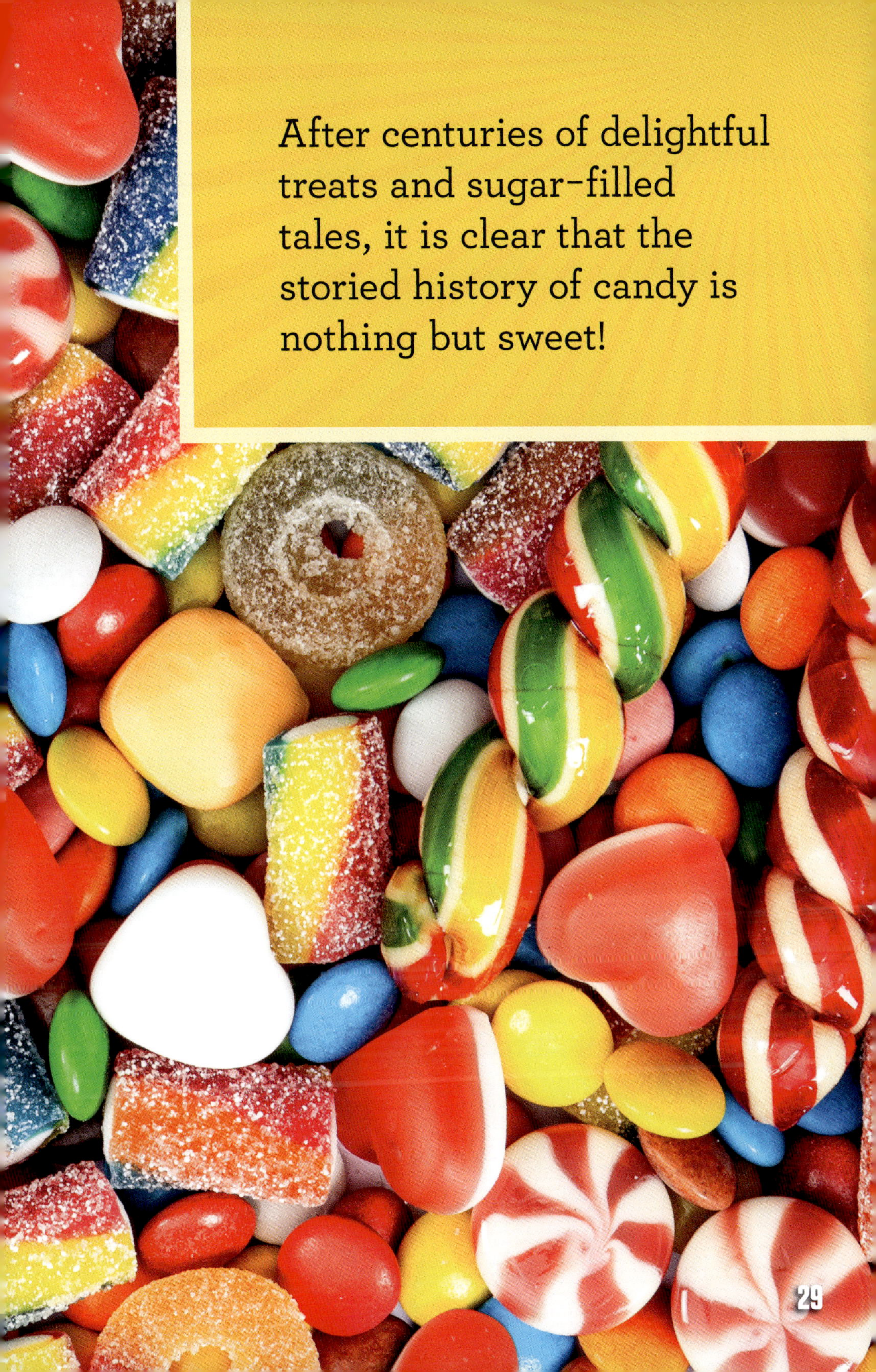

After centuries of delightful treats and sugar-filled tales, it is clear that the storied history of candy is nothing but sweet!

GLOSSARY

confection – a fancy sweet. A confectioner is a person who specializes in making and selling candy or other sweets.

debut – a first appearance.

eco-friendly – not harmful to the environment.

organic – relating to producing foods that are made without the use of laboratory-made fertilizers.

ritual – a religious ceremony with a series of actions.

sustainable – of or related to a method of managing or using a resource so that the resource is never used up.

World War II – (1939–1945) a war fought in Europe, Asia, and Africa. Great Britain, France, the United States, the Soviet Union, and their allies were on one side. Germany, Italy, Japan, and their allies were on the other side.

JUNK FOOD FOR THOUGHT

ONLINE RESOURCES

To learn more about candy, please visit abdobooklinks.com or scan this QR code. These links are routinely monitored and updated to provide the most current information available.

INDEX